LIFE IN THE SEA

Jennifer Coldrey

The Sea

Exploiting the Sea
Exploring the Sea
Food from the Sea
Life in the Sea
The Ocean Floor
Waves, Tides and Currents

Cover picture: A spotted rock cod swims among colourful corals
in a coral reef.

Series editor: Philippa Smith
Editor: Sarah Doughty
Designer: Derek Lee

First published in 1990 by
Wayland (Publishers) Ltd
61 Western Road, Hove
East Sussex BN3 1JD, England

British Library Cataloguing in Publication Data
Coldrey, Jennifer *1940–*
Life in the sea.
1. Oceans. Organisms
I. Title II. Series
574.92

02/9 2   NEL $14.51

ISBN 1 85210 939 4

Phototypeset by Rachel Gibbs, Wayland
Printed and bound in Italy by L.E.G.O. S.p.A., Vicenza

CONTENTS

A West Indian manatee paddles slowly through the inshore waters of the Caribbean.

WHAT LIVES IN THE SEA?

The sea is a vast environment that covers nearly three-quarters of the world's surface. It ranges from the shallow coastal waters around our many islands and continents to the great ocean depths. There are cold polar seas, warm tropical waters and salty inland seas. A huge variety of plants and animals live in the sea but the amount of life in it varies from place to place, depending on the depth and temperature of the water and on how salty it is.

Coral reefs are fertile places where many plants and animals live all year round. In other parts of the sea, life only blooms in the summer months, while in some places nothing lives at all.

Scientists believe that life on Earth first began in the sea. About 3,000 million years ago, tiny plants started to live and grow by feeding on salts and other minerals in the water. Tiny animals then evolved and were able to survive by eating plants.

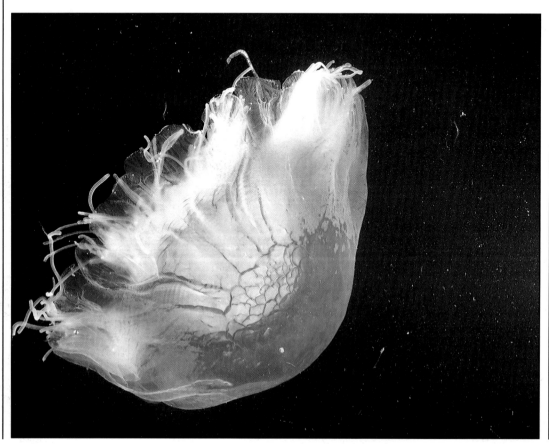

There are many kinds of jellyfish in the sea. This large violet jellyfish is found in North Atlantic waters.

Crabs can be found on the sea-bed at various depths of the ocean. This shore crab is crushing a periwinkle with its pincers.

Even today, sea water can still support life because it contains the nutrients which are needed by plants. The sea also contains dissolved gases, like oxygen, which is needed by both plants and animals for breathing.

Plants also need light in order to grow. So, in the sea, they can survive only in the shallow waters around the coasts and to a depth of about 50 m in the open sea. The plants in the open sea are very different from those on land. They have no roots, stems, leaves or flowers but are simply tiny, free-floating cells that can only be seen under a microscope. They exist in enormous numbers in the upper waters of the oceans and form the basic source of food for all the animals in the sea.

The sea provides a wonderful habitat for many marine animals, including vertebrates such as fish, seals, turtles, penguins and whales. There are also hundreds of fascinating invertebrate animals. These include crabs, lobsters, octopus, squid, jellyfish, sea-urchins, starfish and corals. Each of these marine animals is adapted in its own special way to the part of the sea in which it lives. Some animals float and drift in the surface waters, some swim actively at different levels in the ocean, while others cling, burrow or crawl on the bottom.

The bottle-nosed dolphin, with its smooth, torpedo-shaped body, is a master of speed and agility in the water.

LIFE ON ROCKY SHORES

Around the edges of the continents and islands, the sea meets the land to form the habitat we call the sea-shore. This is a difficult place in which to live because the environment is constantly changing as the tides move in and out each day. Sea-shore plants and animals are constantly battered by the wind and waves. They live in danger of being washed away or of drying out in the sun, and they have to put up with huge and often sudden changes in temperature, as well as changes in the saltiness of the water.

Despite these problems, many plants and animals are well adapted for life on the sea-shore. On rocky shores the large boulders, rocky platforms and rock pools offer excellent places for animals to shelter when the tide is out. Seaweeds can grow on the rocks too. They belong to a group of plants called algae. Unlike land plants, seaweeds do not have roots, but many cling to the rocks with a root-like anchor called a 'holdfast'. Their soft, pliable fronds allow them to bend and sway in the water without breaking. Many seaweeds are covered with slime, which helps

to keep them moist when they are left high and dry at low tide. Different seaweeds live at different levels on the shore. Some of the most delicate species live only in rock pools, while the sturdy brown kelps grow on the lower shore, some below the low water mark.

Different animals live at different levels on the sea-shore, too. Many limpets and barnacles can survive at the top of the shore where they are exposed to the air for long periods of time. When the tide is out, barnacles close

This spiny little squat lobster (not a true lobster) lives among rocks and stones on the lower shore. It uses its huge pincer claws to grasp its food and to defend itself from enemies.

their shells tightly, while limpets clamp their bodies firmly to the rocks with a strong, muscular 'foot'. They emerge to feed only when the tide comes in and covers them again. Many of the sea-shore animals, including sponges, snails, sea squirts and sea anemones, live in rock crevices or under large boulders where they are shaded from the sun at low tide. Crabs, shrimps, sea-urchins and starfish also hide in these places at low tide, while other animals seek shelter among the seaweeds.

Animals in this rock pool include a pink sea-urchin, a starfish, several kinds of sea anemone and the coiled white ribbon of a sea slug's eggs.

Many different kinds of seaweed, some green and some brown, are growing on this rocky shore in Cornwall, Britain.

LIFE ON SANDY AND MUDDY SHORES

On sandy and muddy shores there are no firm surfaces for plants to grow on. Nor are there any rocks or boulders for animals to cling to or hide under. Most of the animals live in burrows or tubes beneath the surface, where they can keep their bodies moist and hidden from danger when the tide is out. Some stay buried all their lives; others, including some shrimps, crabs and starfish, come to the surface to feed when the tide comes in or when it becomes dark.

Some of the most common burrowers are bivalve molluscs, such as cockles, clams and razor-shells. They dig into the sand by pushing out a strong, muscular 'foot' which swells at the end and grips the sand. The animal then pulls its shell-covered body down until it is completely buried. When the tide comes in, these bivalves feed by poking two tubes up above the sand. One tube sucks in sea water containing tiny pieces of food, while the other gets rid of waste.

If you walk along a sandy or muddy beach at low tide, you can often find clues to what is living below. The lugworm, which lives

in a U-shaped burrow in muddy sand, leaves wormcasts on the surface. Close to each cast is a small pit which is made by the worm as it pulls down sand to swallow. The sand passes through its body where any bits of food are digested, and then the remains are pushed out at the surface as a cast. Many other worms live in tubes or burrows. The sand mason and the peacock worm build tubes of sand grains or silt which they glue together with a sticky slime. At low tide they hide inside their tubes, but when the tide comes in they push out a crown of feathery tentacles to catch tiny pieces of food that are in the water.

The large number of wormcasts on this beach in the Galapagos Islands show that there are many lugworms living in the sand.

Muddy shores are especially common in estuaries where the fine-grained silt brought down by the rivers is deposited in the sea. Mud is rich in food and is easier to burrow in than sand. However, it is often short of oxygen and the tiny particles of silt can clog up an animal's gills, making it hard to breathe. Because of this, many mud burrowers have special breathing tubes or comb-like filters which help to keep their gills clean.

Above With the tide in, this common cockle, half-buried in the sand, pushes its feeding tubes into the water.

Left At high tide, peacock worms push out their beautiful fans of tentacles to catch tiny particles of food in the water.

9

LIFE IN SURFACE WATERS

Sunlight can penetrate the sea to a depth of between 50 m and 100 m, depending on how clear the water is. Plants can only grow in these upper, sunlit waters and it is here that many animals are able to flourish too.

Most of the plants are microscopic algae, related to the seaweeds. Some, called diatoms, look like miniature glass boxes. Others have spines or hair-like outgrowths that help them to stay afloat. There are millions of these tiny algae in the upper waters of the sea. Sometimes they multiply so fast that they form a green, brown or red scum on the surface, called a 'bloom'.

Billions of tiny animals live among these algae. They include microscopic star-shaped creatures, and tiny shrimp-like animals called copepods. There are many larger shrimp-like animals, too, as well as worms, floating sea snails and a variety of jellyfish and comb jellies. At certain times of the year these animals are joined by the eggs and larvae of fish, worms, barnacles, starfish, crabs and countless other marine creatures. Together, these tiny plants and animals float and drift in the upper waters of the sea at the mercy of tides and currents. They are called the plankton, a word which comes from the Greek, meaning 'wanderers'.

The Portuguese man-of-war is a sea jelly that drifts at the surface.

Unlike the plants, the animals of the plankton do not need to stay close to the light to survive. Many sink down to lower levels during the day; then at night, when it is cool and dark, they return to the surface to feed on the plants. Some of the plankton animals are carnivorous. These include jellyfish, arrow-worms and shrimps which prey on the other tiny animals.

Larger and more active swimmers also feed in these surface waters. Flying fish, sardines and herrings feast on the plankton. So do the largest fishes of all, the whale sharks and basking sharks, while the huge baleen whales – the largest of all animals – sweep tonnes of plankton into their gigantic mouths.

Smaller fish, such as herrings and anchovies, are in turn eaten by larger fish and by dolphins, seals and penguins which chase after them in the surface waters. There are enemies above the surface, too – hungry sea birds that dive into the sea to snatch up fish and other prey.

Left This shoal of young fish will find plenty of food in the sunlit waters of the sea.

LIFE IN DEEPER WATERS

The deeper one dives into an ocean, the darker and colder it becomes. Below 100 m the light is too dim for plants to grow and the animals live in a sort of twilight world. Most of the animals living at this depth are active swimmers, and many move up to the sunlit waters to feed on plankton or catch small fish. They include plankton-feeders such as prawns, lantern fish, basking sharks and the manta ray.

There are also fast-swimming hunters, including squid, cuttlefish and tuna, as well as predatory sharks and toothed whales that attack and eat fish, turtles and squid. Below about 600 m, no light penetrates the water at all and the ocean is as black as night. The temperature falls close to freezing and there is tremendous pressure from the weight of water above. Very few planktonic animals can live at these depths so larger creatures find food hard to come by. Many animals eat each other. Others eat the waste products and dead remains of animals that drift down from above.

Because of the scarcity of food, most deep-sea fish are fairly small and few grow longer than a human hand. But they make the most of what food they can find, and many are savage predators

Most squid live in deep waters where they hunt for fish and other prey, seizing them with the two long, thin tentacles. This deep-sea species has tiny light organs on its body.

with powerful jaws and needle-sharp teeth. They often have enormous mouths and stomachs which they can stretch when they swallow animals much larger than themselves.

Many fish, prawns and other animals living in mid- and deep-sea waters have luminous patches on their bodies which glow in the dark. Scientists believe that some animals use these lights to attract their prey. Others may use them to confuse their enemies, or to help find a mate and to communicate with others of their kind.

Many deep-sea fish, squid and jellyfish are dark brown or purple in colour, while prawns, shrimps and bristle worms are often deep red or orange. Animals living at the greatest depths, however, are usually pale or almost transparent. There are no strong currents to swim against at these depths, so the fish have poorly developed bones and weak, flabby muscles.

Above A deep-sea angler fish with its luminous fishing lure on its head.

Left This pink and red prawn is typical of deep-water prawns.

A small deep-sea hatchet fish has glowing light organs along the lower sides of its body. It uses its tubular, telescopic eyes to look upwards in search of prey.

LIFE ON THE BOTTOM

The sea-bed is not the same in all parts of the ocean. Around the edges of the continents it is formed by the continental shelf – a gently sloping platform of land which is generally between 80 km and 800 km wide. The shallow seas above this shelf stretch from the tideline to a depth of about 200 m. The floor is covered with layers of mud, sand or gravel washed down from the land by rivers and carried out to sea by tides and currents.

From the edge of the continental shelf the sea-bed drops down a long, steep slope until, at about 4,000 m, it levels out into a deep underwater plain called the abyss. The floor of the slope and the abyss below is very uneven in places, with steep-sided valleys, mountain ridges and long, deep trenches. The floor is mostly mud, but in the deepest parts the sea-bed is covered with a soft, fine ooze which is made up of the tiny skeletons of millions of dead plankton which have sunk to the bottom.

Apart from the seaweeds and one or two other plants that grow in shallow, coastal waters, most of the creatures that live on the bottom are invertebrate animals.

Many, including sponges, corals, barnacles, sea anemones and sea squirts, spend their lives attached to rocks and stones. Others, like crabs, lobsters, prawns, octopus, starfish, sea-urchins and many kinds of marine snails, crawl or creep across the bottom where they prey on other small animals, or scavenge for food. There are lots of burrowing animals too, including many kinds of worms, bivalve molluscs, sea-urchins and starfish. Fish such as cod, haddock and rays cruise along the bottom looking for food in the twilight waters, while flat-fish, like plaice and turbot, lie hidden on the sea-bed.

The sea cucumber is a relative of the starfish and sea-urchin. It moves slowly across the bottom by clinging with its rows of small tube feet. It collects food with its sticky, branched tentacles.

In the deepest and darkest waters, pale crabs and lobsters crawl over the soft mud on long, spindly legs, while ghostly brittle-stars and sea spiders, with legs up to 60 cm long, creep across the bottom. Sea cucumbers are common at these depths and other strange animals – sea pens and sea lilies – stick up from the mud like flowers on long stalks. Fewer species live in these very deep waters but, remarkably, scientists have discovered that some animals, including sea cucumbers and giant tube worms, live around the warm water vents in the deepest ocean trenches. They survive at a depth of over 11,000 m.

Most octopuses live in inshore waters where they lurk among rocks on the sea-bed.

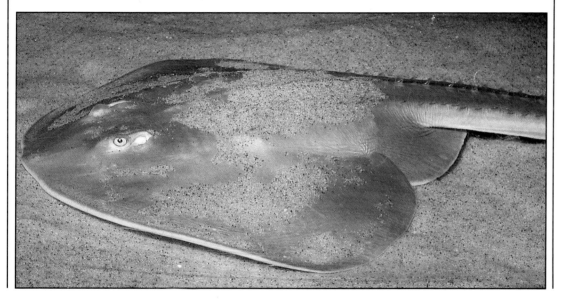

The flattened shape of this thornback ray off the South California coast is ideally suited to moving across the sea-bed. The ray feeds on shrimps, molluscs and other small animals hiding in the sand.

THE FOOD WEB

In the sea, as on land, all animals ultimately depend on plants for their food. Plants can use the energy from sunlight to make their own food from simple chemicals and gases in a process called photosynthesis. Animals cannot make their own food; they need to eat plants or other animals in order to live and grow. In the sea, it is the billions of tiny plants in the plankton that provide the basic food supply for other marine creatures. The seaweeds around the coasts also provide food for some marine animals, such as sea-urchins, winkles and limpets.

Many small animals in the plankton feed on the plant plankton. Other animals, including fish such as sardines and anchovies, feed on it, too. The small planktonic animals are in turn eaten by larger, carnivorous animals, including planktonic creatures like shrimps and jellyfish, and active hunters like herrings, mackerel, basking sharks and the great baleen whales which feed mainly on small shrimps called krill. Small fish such as herrings and mackerel are in turn eaten by bigger fish, or by predators like seals, penguins, sea birds, sharks and killer whales.

In this way, food and energy are passed on from plants to small animals, and then to larger animals, through what we call a food chain. Some food chains are short and simple; for example, a green turtle eats seaweed, or a blue whale eats krill, which eats animal plankton, which in turn, eats plant plankton. But other food chains are longer and more complicated, and there may be many other cross-links between different animals. As a result the food chains become woven into a food web. We, as human beings, interfere with the food web in the

A fisherman with crayfish pots in Australia. The amount of marine life taken out of the sea must be carefully controlled so the food web is not harmed too seriously.

sea by catching fish, crabs and other marine animals to eat. It is very important that we try not to upset the delicate balance of marine life – overfishing can remove too many animals of one kind from the sea.

Of course some animals and plants are never eaten. They eventually die and fall to the bottom of the sea. Their remains are devoured by scavengers, or they rot away, as bacteria breaks down their bodies into simple chemicals. Small particles of food are snapped up by filter feeders like tube worms and barnacles, while the minerals released into the sea are eventually brought up to the surface by the upwelling currents and then are used again by the planktonic plants.

Part of a marine food web. The bold arrows point from the predators to their prey.

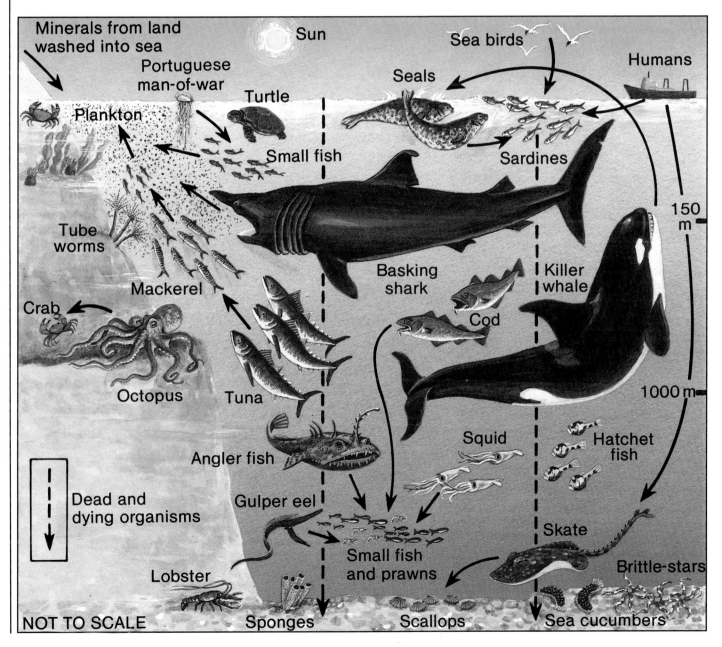

17

CORAL REEFS

Coral reefs are found in warm, shallow seas in tropical regions of the world. One of the largest and most famous is the Great Barrier Reef off the north-east coast of Australia. It is some 2,000 km long and, from space, looks like a gigantic wall on the face of the Earth.

A coral reef is in fact a mass of hard, limestone skeletons built by thousands of tiny marine animals – corals. Although many corals look like plants, they are actually colonies of little animals closely related to sea anemones. The body of a single coral animal is called a polyp. It is a soft, tube-like creature, attached to the bottom at one end and with a ring of tentacles around its mouth at the other end. Like a sea anemone, it uses its tentacles to catch tiny animals in the water. Every coral starts its life as one polyp. Some stay as single animals, but most reef corals grow and divide to form huge colonies of connected polyps. The soft body of each polyp is protected by a hard outer case or skeleton. As old polyps die new ones grow on top of them, but the old skeletons remain and so the coral reef grows higher and higher.

There are well over 350 species of coral on the Great Barrier Reef and their varied shapes and

The parrot fish uses its hard, beak-like jaws to bite off chunks of living coral.

colours are wonderful to see. Living in and among these corals are a wealth of other animals and plants. Tiny algae live inside the polyps and provide the corals with extra food. Other kinds of algae grow on the dead and empty parts of the reef. Attached to the corals are animals such as sponges, tube worms, sea anemones, barnacles and clams. Slow-moving creatures like sea snails, flatworms, sea slugs and starfish creep across the corals to search for food, while crabs, shrimps, worms and a host of colourful fish come to find food or to make their homes on the coral reef.

Some of these animals actually feed on the coral polyps. Parrot fish have sharp, beak-like jaws which they use to crush the hard coral to get at the soft polyps inside. Many other reef fish have mouths and teeth that are specially adapted for cutting, probing or rasping at the coral.

The large crown of thorns starfish is a serious pest on coral reefs as it sucks out the polyps.

Perched among colourful corals and encrusting algae, a large sea anemone waves its tentacles in warm, tropical water.

THE SARGASSO SEA

The Sargasso Sea is a strange and fascinating part of the western Atlantic Ocean, first discovered by Christopher Columbus in 1492. It is an area of warm, still water surrounded by a ring of currents. The currents flow in a clockwise direction, and inside their huge circle the deep, blue waters are calm and clear. Floating on the surface are large clumps of brown seaweed called Sargassum weed. This living seaweed originally came from pieces that broke away from plants growing along the shores of Central America and the islands of the Caribbean. The weed is kept afloat by its round, berry-like floats.

The Sargassum weed provides a home and shelter for a variety of animals. Barnacles, tube worms, sea anemones and sponges live permanently attached to it, while many fronds are encrusted with white lacy growths formed by colonies of moss animals, also called sea mats. Tiny, branching hydroids, some only 1 mm tall, also grow on the weed. They stand out stiffly in the water where their stubby tentacles filter tiny scraps of food from the sea.

Flatworms, ragworms and sea slugs creep over the weed, while

Large clumps of golden-brown Sargassum weed float on the surface of the Sargasso Sea.

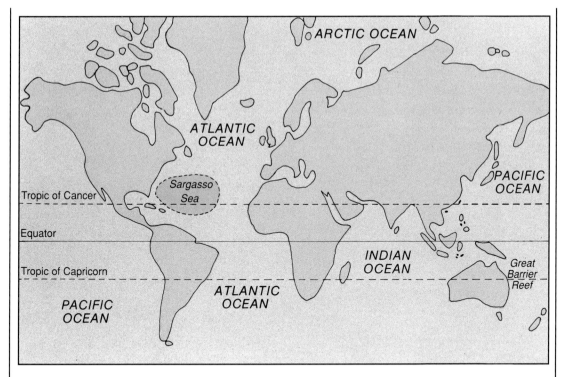

The Sargasso Sea is a region of the Atlantic Ocean. It gets its name from the Sargassum weed.

shrimps, crabs and several kinds of fish find food and shelter among the fronds. Flying fish come to lay their eggs in cocoon-like nests hidden among the weed. Here the young larvae can grow in safety until they are old enough to slip away into the open sea. The Sargassum weed also provides a nursery for baby eels before they set out on their amazing journeys across the Atlantic Ocean. Other visitors to the Sargasso Sea include pilot fish, dolphin fish, small squid and the occasional jellyfish.

Many of the more permanent residents are carnivorous. Rather than feeding on the weed that shelters them, they eat each other. To improve their chances of survival, many of the animals rely on camouflage to hide from their enemies. Most shrimps, crabs and sea slugs are very hard to spot amongst the weed, but the real master of disguise is the Sargassum angler fish, a fearsome predator which eats mainly shrimps. Its body has wispy outgrowths of skin and is coloured and patterned to blend in perfectly with the weed. It stalks its prey by creeping through the weed with hand-like fins which grip the fronds.

The tiny Sargassum crab is no bigger than a pea. Its body is well camouflaged among the Sargassum weed.

FISH OF THE SEA

There are thousands of different kinds of fish in the sea. They come in a huge variety of shapes, sizes and colours, ranging from the silvery flying fish which leap in and out of the waves in tropical seas to the bottom-living rays and other curious flatfish.

Fish are well adapted to life in the sea, being able to breathe underwater using their gills. They take in water through their mouth and then pass it out through their gills, where oxygen from the water is absorbed into their bloodstream. Fish also have special senses to help them find their way underwater. Along each side of the body is a row of nerves, called the lateral line, which can sense vibrations in the water. The signals it receives warn the fish of any obstacles or moving creatures in the water nearby, helping it to avoid danger or to find food more easily.

The bodies of most fish are ideally suited for movement through water. They have a smooth, streamlined shape, tapering at each end, and their various fins help them to balance and steer. The fastest swimmers have the smoothest outline and their strong muscular bodies and a crescent-shaped tail help to drive them along. These fish include high-speed hunters like mackerel, large tuna, sailfish, swordfish, and predatory sharks.

Sharks are fast-moving hunters, with powerful, flexible bodies. This grey reef shark is chasing after a shoal of small fish.

The sea-horse is a rather unusual kind of fish. It lives in shallow, warm seas and feeds by sucking up tiny shrimps and other animals through its long tube-like snout.

The bodies of some fish are coloured to make them less obvious to potential attackers. Many of the smaller fish live in enormous shoals which helps to protect them from predators. As a shoal twists and turns like one body in the water, the silvery sides of the fish reflect the light, dazzling and confusing their enemies. There are other forms of protective colouring, too. Many fish of the open sea are dark green or blue on the back but pale underneath. This means that birds and other enemies above cannot see them so clearly against the dark sea below, while predators beneath find them difficult to see against the sunlit waters above. Flatfish such as plaice and flounders are camouflaged in a different way. Their upper sides are speckled and blotched with colours which blend in beautifully with the sea-bed on which they lie.

The mottled skin of a plaice changes colour so that it cannot be seen on the sea-bed.

MAMMALS OF THE SEA

Mammals cannot breathe underwater, so those that live in the sea have to come to the surface regularly for air. The smallest sea mammal is the sea otter, a furry animal about 1 m long, which lives close to the shore along parts of the North Pacific coast. It is an excellent swimmer and diver, with a streamlined body, powerful tail and two broad, fully-webbed back feet which it uses like paddles.

Seals, sea lions and walruses are another group of furry sea mammals. They are found in many parts of the world, especially in colder seas. Their smooth, torpedo-shaped bodies are well adapted for swimming and diving, and in place of legs they have paddle-like flippers. Seals and sea lions are active hunters and feed by chasing after fish, squid and shellfish. They spend most of their lives at sea, but have to come ashore, or on to ice floes, to mate and give birth.

The mammals best adapted for life at sea are the whales. These giant creatures never leave the sea, even giving birth and suckling their young underwater. The whales' front limbs are flippers but their back limbs have

disappeared altogether, giving the animals a fish-like shape. There is a horizontal two-finned 'fluke' at the end of the tail which helps to drive the whale through the water. Some whales also have a fin on their back. Like all mammals, whales have lungs. They breathe by coming to the surface where they blow out the stale air and suck in fresh air through the blowhole on top of their head.

There are two main groups of whales. There are the toothed whales, which include dolphins, porpoises and killer whales, and the baleen whales, such as the grey, blue and humpback whales. Toothed whales use their small,

A diver swims close to a pilot whale in the sea. Pilot whales are members of the dolphin family and are usually to be found in large groups.

peg-like teeth to help catch fish and squid. Some toothed whales dive very deep in search of their prey, while baleen whales feed nearer the surface on small planktonic animals. Instead of teeth they have rows of horny 'whalebone' plates hanging down from their upper jaws. The inner edges of these plates are frayed into a fringe of coarse, bristly hairs which act like a sieve. As the whale takes in a mouthful of plankton, the tiny animals are trapped in this sieve while the water flows out through the plates at the sides of its mouth.

One other strange group of sea mammals are the dugongs and manatees. They live in tropical inshore waters where they feed on seaweeds and other marine plants. They are slow, bulky

A South Australian sea lion has a scratch with its back flipper before returning to the sea for a swim.

animals with paddle-shaped front limbs, no hind limbs and a flattened, horizontal tail fluke. They give birth under water and spend their whole lives in the sea.

A sea otter floats on its back while eating a sea-urchin.

SEA BIRDS

Many birds depend on the sea for their food even though they nest and rear their young on land. Most of these 'sea birds' have webbed feet and a well-oiled, waterproof plumage, which enables them to swim and dive for food. Some sea birds like gulls, cormorants and pelicans stay close to the land for most of their lives, fishing in the sea and returning to the land at night to sleep. Others, including penguins, albatrosses and auks, spend most of their lives out at sea and only come ashore at certain times of the year to mate and breed.

Among the birds which feed in inshore waters close to land are gulls and terns, sea ducks like the eider, which feed mainly on mussels and crabs, and the cormorants and shags, which dive down from the surface to hunt for fish. When the tide is out, a variety of wading birds, such as turnstones, dunlin, oystercatchers and curlews, can be seen on many shores, searching under stones and seaweed or probing into the sand and mud for worms, shrimps and molluscs.

Further out to sea, gannets and boobies, some terns, and auks like the puffins, razorbills and guillemots, feed in deeper waters, often sleeping on the water at night. The auks dive from the surface to feed, using their short stubby wings as paddles to help them swim and catch fish, squid and worms. Gannets and terns dive down from above the water to catch their prey. Gannets are a spectacular sight as they plunge like arrows into the sea, their sharp, heavy beaks ready to spear the fish below.

Furthest out in the open sea live the ocean-going albatrosses, as well as shearwaters and petrels. Albatrosses can soar for hundreds of kilometres on their huge outstretched wings. They often glide low over the water, hunting for fish, squid and shrimps.

Oystercatchers are a common sight on many sea-shores at low tide. They use their heavy red bills to hammer or prise open mussels, oysters and other shellfish to get at the soft flesh inside.

Shearwaters and petrels are smaller birds which also travel widely. They skim over the waves in search of small fish just beneath the surface.

Of all sea birds penguins are the best adapted for life at sea. Their plump, streamlined bodies are covered by closely-packed water-proof feathers, and instead of wings they have strong flippers. Although they look rather clumsy on land, penguins are agile in the water, swimming and diving with amazing speed and skill to catch fish, squid and krill.

Above The wandering albatross is the largest of all sea birds and a superb glider.

Left These chinstrap penguins breed on islands and shores around Antarctica. Their thick plumage and layers of fat help them to survive in the freezing waters.

JOURNEYS AND MIGRATIONS

Some marine animals, such as corals, barnacles and mussels, stay fixed to one spot on the sea-bed all their lives. Others are free to move about in the sea. Drifting plankton may be carried long distances by ocean currents, while creatures that swim and crawl can move actively from place to place in search of food, to find a mate or to escape from enemies.

Many of the larger animals make regular journeys, or migrations, at certain times of the year to look for food or to find a suitable place to breed. Penguins, turtles and seals all make long journeys from the sea on to land to lay eggs or give birth to their young on special breeding grounds. Baleen whales also make long migrations, travelling as far as 8,000 km each year. In summer they feed on the rich supplies of krill and other plankton in the polar seas, and then they migrate to warmer, tropical waters for the winter to breed and nurse their young.

After a long journey at sea, the female leathery turtle comes ashore at night to lay her eggs in the sand at the top of the beach.

Many fish migrate to different parts of the sea to spawn. Herrings, for example, move into coastal waters where the females shed many thousands of eggs into the sea. The eggs hatch into larvae which are carried by currents to sheltered waters that are rich in food. Here they grow and develop until, at two or three years old, they move out to deeper waters to join the adult shoals.

The most remarkable fish migrations are those of eels and salmon. European and American eels spend their adult life in freshwater lakes, ponds and rivers. When it is time to breed they move downstream to the sea and migrate across the Atlantic Ocean to the Sargasso Sea. From parts of Europe this is a journey of some 5,000 km and no one knows quite how long it takes.

After spawning in the Sargasso Sea the adults probably die. But the eggs hatch into tiny, transparent leaf-shaped larvae which eventually make the long journey back across the Atlantic. It takes a year for the American eel larvae to reach the eastern coast of North America, while European eel larvae take up to three years to find their way home. By the time they reach the coasts and start to move upstream, they look like tiny eels and are called elvers. Salmon and sea trout migrate in the opposite direction. They spend their adult lives at sea, but swim up rivers to spawn in freshwater streams. The young salmon stay in the rivers for one to five years before migrating out to sea. When the fish are ready to spawn they find their way back to the river in which they were born.

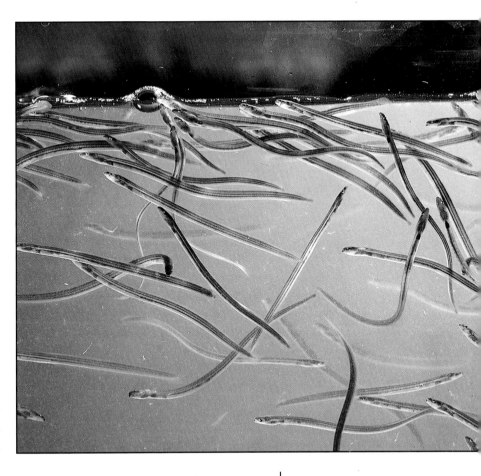

These young elvers, having migrated across the Atlantic Ocean from the Sargasso Sea, now move upstream in an English river.

A group of adult Atlantic salmon start their journey from the sea to spawn in the freshwater river where they were born.

GLOSSARY

Abyss The deepest part of the ocean, between 4,000 m and 6,000 m down.

Adapted Changed so as to become better suited to a particular way of life.

Algae Simple plants without proper roots, leaves or flowers. Seaweeds are algae, as are the microscopic plants in the plankton.

Auks A family of sea birds which includes puffins, razorbills and guillemots.

Bacteria Microscopic organisms (neither plants nor animals) which are found everywhere and help to rot down dead animals and plants.

Baleen Thin, horny plates (also called whalebonc) which are found in the mouths of baleen whales and are used to filter food, mainly plankton, from the sea.

Bivalve A type of mollusc with a hinged double shell. Mussels, cockles, clams and oysters are all bivalves.

Camouflage A form of disguise which helps an animal to blend in with its background so that it cannot easily be seen by its enemies.

Carnivorous Meat-eating; feeding on other animals.

Cell The basic unit from which all living things are made up. Most cells are microscopic.

Continental shelf The underwater platform of land that juts out into the sea around continents.

Environment The surroundings in which plants and animals live.

Estuary The wide mouth of a river where it flows into the sea.

Evolve To change and develop over a long period of time and through many generations as a result of adaptations to the environment.

Fertile Rich in nutrients.

Flukes The horizontal tail fins of whales.

Fronds The branches of a plant.

Gills Branched or comb-like structures which most underwater animals use to absorb oxygen from the water for breathing.

Habitat The place in which an animal or plant lives.

Hydroid A branching colony of tiny polyps, related to sea anemones and jellyfish.

Invertebrates Animals without backbones.

Krill Small, shrimp-like animals which are abundant in the plankton of polar seas.

Larva (plural: larvae) A young stage in the life of many marine animals. Larvae hatch from eggs and are often very different from the adult forms into which they develop.

Mammals Warm-blooded animals with hair or fur which feed their young on milk. Seals, whales and humans are all mammals.

Marine Of, found in, or belonging to the sea (fish are marine animals).

Migration A regular journey made by animals at certain times of the year, to find food, to survive the winter or to find a place to breed.

Molluscs A large group of soft-bodied animals which includes slugs, snails, octopus, squid and bivalves.

Nutrients Substances in food which provide nourishment, so helping animals and plants to grow and remain healthy.

Ooze The soft, fine-grained mud at the bottom of the oceans, made from the skeletons of tiny planktonic creatures.

Photosynthesis The process by which plants make food from simple chemicals using the energy from sunlight.

Plankton Plants and animals which float and drift in the upper waters of the sea.

Plumage A bird's feathers.

Predator An animal that kills and eats other animals for food.

Prey An animal that is killed and eaten by another animal.

Scavenger An animal that feeds on dead plants and animals.

Shoal A large number of fish swimming together.

Spawn To lay eggs in the water.

Species A particular kind of plant or animal that is unlike all other kinds and which can only breed successfully with its own kind.

Streamlined Having a smooth, slender shape which does not block the flow of air or water.

Tropical A word describing the warm regions of the world to the north and south of the Equator.

Vertebrates Animals with backbones.

BOOKS TO READ

The Crab on the Seashore by Jennifer Coldrey (Methuen, 1986)
Jellyfish and Other Sea Jellies by Jennifer Coldrey (Deutsch, 1981)
The Nature Trail Book of Seashore Life by Su Swallow (Usborne, 1976)
Protecting the Oceans by John Baines (Wayland, 1990)
Seas and Oceans by David Lambert (Wayland, 1987)
Seashore Animals (The Clue Books) by Gwen Allen and Joan Denslow (Oxford University Press, 1972)
Whales by Noel Simon (Dent, 1981)
The Young Geographer Investigates Oceans and Seas by Terry Jennings (Oxford University Press, 1988)
The Young Scientist Investigates Sea and Seashore by Terry Jennings (Oxford University Press, 1988)

For older readers:

Collins Pocket Guide to the Seashore by J. H. Barrett and C. M. Yonge (Collins, 1984)
The Guinness Book of Seashore Life by Heather Angel (Guideway, 1981)
The Living World of the Sea by Bernard Stonehouse (Hamlyn, 1979)

INDEX

Picture Acknowledgements

Bruce Coleman Ltd *cover* (Allan Power), 4 (Jane Burton), 6 (Jane Burton), 8 (Konrad Wothe), 9 both (Jane Burton), 14 (Jane Burton), 18 (Carl Roessler), 25 bottom (Frans Lanting), 26 (Gunter Zeisler), 28 (Jane Burton), 29 top (Jane Burton); Frank Lane Picture Agency 22, 27 bottom; Oxford Scientific Films 5 top (G.I Bernard) and bottom (Warwick Johnson), 11 both (Peter Parks), 15 top (Laurence Gould), 20 (Peter Parks), 21 (Peter Parks); Seaphot Ltd/Planet Earth Pictures 7 top (David George) and bottom (Julian Partridge), 10 (Andrew Mounter), 12 (Peter David), 13 top (Peter David), middle (Peter David) and bottom (Norbert Wu), 15 bottom (Ken Lucas), 19 top (Ken Lucas) and bottom (Nancy Sefton), 23 top (Georgette Douwma) and bottom (John Lythgoe), 24 (James D. Watt), 25 top (Debbie Perrin), 27 top (Julian Hector), 29 bottom (Gilbert van Ryckevorsel); Survival Anglia *contents page;* Wayland Picture Library 16. The artwork on page 17 is by Wendy Meadway; page 21 is by Marilyn Clay. Cover and title page artwork by John Yates.